CW00841637

How To Freelance Writer

Your Step–By–Step Guide To Becoming a Freelance Writer

HowExpert with Chelsea Hammond

Copyright HowExpert™
www.HowExpert.com

For more tips related to this topic, visit www.HowExpert.com/writing.

Recommended Resources

www.HowExpert.com – Quick 'How To' Guides on Unique Topics by Everyday Experts.

www.HowExpert.com/writers - Write About Your #1 Passion/Knowledge/Experience.

www.HowExpert.com/membership - Learn a New 'How To' Topic About Practically Everything Every Week.

www.HowExpert.com/jobs - Check Out HowExpert Jobs.

Table of Contents

How To Be A Freelance Writer

So, you have found the world of freelance writing, and you think that it might be something you would like to do. Otherwise, why would you have purchased and began to read this book, right? You are in luck, because in a few very simple steps, I will tell you how to go about becoming a freelance writer. It's fairly simple to do. The most difficult part is figuring out where you need to start, and that is why I am here.

Of course, these days, there a lot more people who are following their artistic dreams. This is because it has become easier than ever to do so in this time of modern technology. Don't be fooled into thinking that it is only musicians and artists who are getting more freedom, however. Writers, also, have been given more freedom to do what they enjoy doing - which, of course, is writing. If you have a true passion for writing, or a strong desire to have your words be read by the general public, you have come to the right place.

Almost anyone can become a freelance writer, and these writers can work everywhere. For today's purposes, however, we are going to show you how to do your freelance writing at home, through the Internet. As long as you are able to spell, use a computer, and finagle your way through the worldwide web, you will be able to do everything I teach you today. I am here to not only to teach you how to become a freelance writer, but also to explain the different types of freelance writing there are out there right now. Hopefully, any questions you may currently have will be answered by the time you have finished reading this.

Chapter 1 - Making Sure You Have Everything You Need

This step is fairly simple, and odds are that you already have everything you need to get started. If you don't, these materials are all fairly inexpensive. That is, besides the computer, which is the one thing I am sure, at least, you already own.

You begin with a computer and a reliable internet connection. Any computer will do - a laptop, a desk top - it doesn't matter. Now, what do I mean by a reliable internet connection? I mean a connection that you own, and that you know will not go out on you, that you can access 24 hours a day, 7 days a week. This doesn't mean a Wi-Fi hotspot that you can sometimes connect to and sometimes can't. This also doesn't mean an extremely slow connection, as this will cause the amount of time it takes you to do a certain task a lot longer, and thus, drop your productivity level. I suggest some type of DSL or other high-speed connection. It shouldn't cost you more than $60 a month, and if you work hard, you will make that, and much more, in a single month of freelance writing work.

Next, you will need pens or pencils and some paper. Notepads or loose paper will do the job just fine. Chances are, sticky notes would even do the job for you if that's all you have at the moment. Mostly, you need your writing utensils and paper to take quick notes, or to remind yourself of something you must do, in case you don't log onto the computer during the time you need to be reminded. Just about all of your work will be done on the computer itself, via some type of application (mostly Microsoft Word), so the pen and paper is just something that is good to have handy.

As for computer software, you should only need Microsoft Word or another similar application. A really great free word processing program is called Open Office, and it can be downloaded online at no cost to you. Open Office contains all of the things that you would get if you purchased a Microsoft Office Package - text documents, spreadsheets, the whole works. If you really wanted to go the extra mile, then you could also download or purchase some type of article spinning software, as there are a few jobs that will require it. If you don't want to do these types of jobs, then there is no reason for you to spend any extra money on the software. In fact, there are still a good number of employers who prefer articles to be "hand-spun" versus "software-spun."

You will also need to get on Skype. Even if you don't have a video camera hooked up to your computer, you can still use Skype, and it's free. This isn't a must, but it is something I highly recommend. This will enable your employers to call you or chat with you, no matter where you are currently located in relation to where they are currently located. Whether or not you end up setting yourself up with a Skype account, you will still need some type of instant messaging service. Aim and Yahoo are two major instant messengers that a lot of people still use today. These types of instant messengers, however, are becoming fairly obsolete, so I still suggest using Skype.

Last, but not least, you will need an email address. Preferably, this will be an email address that you use strictly for work. If you have to create a new one, in addition to your personal email account, that's fine. Email is free and there are plenty of places that you can get an email address if you don't already, or if you want to set one up specifically for your freelance writing. While you can use your personal account as your business account, it is easier to find emails you are looking for if you keep the two separate. It helps you to keep things just a little bit more organized. Just the tiniest bit of extra organization can help make your life a whole lot simpler.

That's it. That is all you need to get started. Most people these days will have every last one of those items. So, once you make sure you have everything on the list, you are ready to move on to the next step along the road to freelance writing. Just make sure that everything is in a place where you will remember where it is, and where all of your materials are close at hand.

Chapter 2 – Know What You Are Talking About

Freelance writers use a lot of slang terms that are pretty much exclusive to the industry. A few of these, you will never need to know, or you can learn as you go. But I'm going to go ahead and get you started with a few basic terms that every freelance writer needs to know. In addition, I will add in a few basic "text" items that you should probably already know. Just in case you don't, however, I will mention them, since they will come up at least a few times in your freelance writing career.

IM - This stands for "Instant Message." If someone tells you to "IM" them, it means that you need to message them on an instant messenger service. Usually they will tell you which one, and if they do not, then you need only ask.

PM - This stands for "Private Message." The difference between this and IM is that you would usually privately message them through the online platform you are using, or else through an email, versus an instant messaging application.

SEO - Ah, now here is a really big one, folks. SEO stands for "Search Engine Optimization." If you know what that means, than it is pretty much self explanatory. This abbreviation refers to the use of keywords placed in website content or articles in order to help the aforementioned website or article rank high in the search engines. The higher the keyword density, the more often the site or article or blog or whatever it is will show up in the search engine results. Just for clarity, search engines are places like Google, Yahoo, and Bing where you can type in what you want to find in a search bar and a whole list of sites and web pages show up. But I'm fairly sure you already knew that.

Copy - Copy refers to writing materials that are used on websites, billboards, and other advertisements for strictly marketing purposes. "Copy" is meant to sell something or to persuade someone to a specific idea, opinion, or way of thinking. Sometimes you will see that people want "copy" that is not meant to sell anything, but this is often either a misuse of the term, or else is a non-profit organization, in which case they are trying to persuade people to a specific opinion as I mentioned before.

Pvs - This stands for "Page Views." Page views are the number of times that an article or a collection of articles has been viewed in a specifically allotted amount of time. Basically, this shows how much "traffic" a page has gotten.

Traffic - Just in case you didn't already know, traffic does not refer to the number of cars parked outside of your window while you are working. Instead, it refers to the number of people who are on a specific website or web page at a certain time or during a certain time period. Basically, it is the same thing as page views, only in a much broader sense.

CPC - This stands for "cost per click." This is the cost to the advertiser for each time someone clicks on an ad.

PPM - This means "Pay Per Thousand." I know, where did the 'm' come from then? The "M" in "PPM" refers to the Roman numeral for one thousand. The PPM is the estimated amount of money that a writer will receive for every one thousand page views.

Affiliate Marketing - Affiliate Marketing refers to the process of companies paying people to place online links to their products. Practically all online businesses use this form of marketing, as it is fairly simple, straight-forward, and (usually) inexpensive.

ASAP - This is an abbreviation for "As Soon As Possible." It means exactly what it sounds like- whatever they want you to do, they want you to do it as quickly as you possibly can.

FYI - Another abbreviation. This one means "For Your Information." Someone is about to fill you in on something.

TY - "Thank You." Someone is being abruptly polite.

YW - "You're Welcome" or "You are Welcome," but then again, it's all the same thing in the end, isn't it?

Newbie - A "Newbie" refers to a person who is just beginning their freelance writing career. They have no formal skills or training. A lot of people will ask only for newbies in a job posting, because they are offering training. Other job postings will state that they do not want any newbies applying to the job, and this means that the job requires a certain amount of skill or knowledge.

WPM - This stands for "Words Per Minute." This is the number of words that you can type accurately in one minute. A good WPM goal to shoot for is between 40 and 50. The more, the better, of course, as this increases your productivity and enables you to get jobs done more quickly. I type around 60 wpm on average, and I am always striving to increase that. When I first began my freelance writing career, I only typed around 35 to 40 wpm. There is always room for improvement if you want there to be.

Bidding - Bidding refers to applying for a job, but more specifically, it is the amount of money you have said that you will do the job for. When you apply for a job, you must make a "bid" or name an amount of compensation you would like upon completion or at the end of each week.

Outbid - When you "outbid" someone, you place a lower bid than another contractor. Often, the person with the lowest or most affordable bid has a higher chance of getting the job.

Gig - This is a fairly widely used slang term that means "job." It is one of the few slang terms that are usually appropriate in business related circumstances.

Pitch - A "pitch" is when a writer is trying to sell their idea for an article or project to an editor or a client. This is sometimes also called a "query." Both words mean that exact same thing.

Portfolio - A portfolio is a website, booklet, or listing that shows all of the best work from a specific writer.

Your own portfolio will show your best work in a way that is easily accessible to perspective clients.

On a final note, if you are ever not sure what someone is saying, there are two things you could do. (1) You could simply politely ask whoever it is you are talking to what they are saying, or (2) you could look it up in the search engines. I will bet my bottom dollar that you will be able to find it in the search engines, and you will not have to feel as though the person you are talking to thinks you are "stupid" because you didn't know what they were talking about.

Chapter 3 - The Freelance Writing Myths

I know that there are a lot of myths out there about freelancing writing, and just so you know, almost none of them are true. I'm going to list a few of them, and although this book is based solely on how to become a freelancer online, a few of these myths also apply to freelancing out in the real world.

Myth #1: You must have a college degree in order to do freelance writing.

This is so far from the truth, it's not even funny. I, myself, do not have a college degree and I have never had any problem doing freelance work. Anyone who possesses basic writing skills, has a strong desire to learn, and a fierce determination to get ahead in life can become a freelance writer.

Myth #2: Only stay-at-home-moms do work-at-home jobs.

These days, there are a very large number of people who work from home. This doesn't just apply to the writing industry, either, but to many, many other industries.

Myth #3: You must start out your freelance writing career writing obituaries.

Honestly, I had never heard this one, but I did find it on a whole lot of blogs dedicated to freelance writing. The answer, of course, is that you do not have to start out your freelance writing career writing obituaries. You can start your career in any way you so desire. I mean, if you want to write obituaries, then fine, go ahead. If not, then don't fret, because any person who tells you this is just full of it.

Myth #4: You will have plenty of free time if you become a freelance writer.

I'm sorry to burst your bubble, but wrong again. It is true that you are able to make your own schedule in almost all circumstances, but that doesn't mean you have all of the free time in the world. If you are serious about being a freelance writer, then you will still have to put plenty of time into it.

Myth #5: You must have connections in order to begin your career.

Nope, this is also false. I, personally, have no connections whatsoever, and I make a very small fortune every year doing freelance writing. The only "connection" you actually need is an internet connection.

Myth #6: Online writing jobs do not pay as much as print ones.

Wow, this one actually makes me laugh. It isn't even close to the truth. In fact, I do all of my freelance writing exclusively online, and I have never had any problems making enough money to get by. In fact, some of the jobs I've had paid pretty well. You may not be able to make a fortune overnight, but you will be able to make plenty of money doing online freelancing if you put your mind to it.

Myth #7: You need technical knowledge in order to freelance online.

Not even close. In fact, the only "technical knowledge" you actual need to have is the ability to use email and use a search engine to its fullest capabilities. Oh, and you need to have basic word-processing skills (think Microsoft Word and Open Office), which is taught to middle schoolers these days. Honestly, it wouldn't surprise me if, in today's world, a five year old possessed all of the "technical knowledge" to become a freelance writer.

Myth #8: You must live in the United States in order to become a successful freelance writer.

There are plenty of successful freelancers from all over the world, who speak all different languages. I, personally, have worked for people located in the United Kingdom, Australia, and Canada. I have competed for jobs against people in Asia and the Middle East. You can live anywhere in the world and do freelancing successfully. To be perfectly honest, if there was an internet connection on the moon, you could work up there and still be a successful freelancer.

Myth #9: Anyone can write.

Well, this one is half true. Anyone can write, but not everyone can write well. Everyone can, however, learn to write well, which is why I stress educating yourself whenever you get the chance.

Myth #10: Blogging is not really writing.

Blogging really is writing. In fact, it is one of the most widely recognized ways of writing these days, and blogs all around the world are now routinely getting turned into books, or are used to market new products. True, it seems like everyone has a blog these days, and so it would be assumed that everyone can be a successful, published writer. Yet just as in books, movies, and music - there are good bloggers, there are mediocre bloggers, and then there are terrible bloggers. Thus is life.

Myth #11: Freelance writers are not reliable.

There are a few unreliable freelance writers out there, and sadly, they have ruined it for many clients. This is a stereotypical generalization, however, and most freelance writers are very reliable. It just depends on the person themselves. So make sure that you are always reliable, and don't give all freelancers a bad name.

Myth #12: Writers need to have a huge vocabulary and perfect grammar.

No, this is what the dictionary and thesaurus are for. As I've already said before, it's better to be educated, which includes on topics like vocabulary and grammar, but it isn't necessary.

Chapter 4 - Deciding Which Type Of Freelancer You Want To Be

There are a lot of people who believe all writing is the same. If someone can do one type of writing, then they should be able to do all other types. Yet this is a stereotype, and one which is far from true. Just like a person who plays the bass guitar can't necessarily play the drums and keyboard as well, a person who does content writing can't necessarily do article writing or become an indie author as well. If you don't already know which type of freelance writing you do best, or which type you would enjoy doing the best, then feel free to try a few different things out. Eventually, you will find your niche, or figure out your own abilities.

Now that you know you don't necessarily have to do all work or be good at every type of freelance writing, let's talk about the choices there are in this field. Remember: you don't have to choose just one. Many of these fields go hand in hand with others, and there are people out there who can do all of it, and perfectly! You may decide that you can do everything but technical writing, or that you can only do technical writing. Never be embarrassed that you must specialize in only one or two categories because the skills necessary to do the others elude you. You are your own person. Remember that everything depends on you, and don't let anyone put you down because of what you can or cannot do in regards to freelance writing (or anything else, for that matter).

Now, on with the business at hand. Let's discuss the types of writing available to you.

Copy Writing

Copy writing refers to the act of writing content that is meant exclusively for advertisement or promotional purposes. It can be done in order to advertise or promote a person, web site, product, gig, opinion, idea, etc. Often a person who does "copy writing" will also do "content writing" as the two jobs go hand in hand with one another.

People who work in the copy writing field will have various types of jobs. These may include, but are certainly not limited to: writing website content, product descriptions, category and/or page descriptions, press releases, email advertisements, promotional skits meant for phone, email, or video, online ads, and various other types of marketing communications writing.

People who have previous sales experience, or who are good at knowing what people (as a whole, and as a consumer) want to hear, might do well in this field. Additional things that you should know, or aim to learn, are SEO, social media marketing, and, as always when you are working with computers, a basic knowledge of HTML and computer functions. This doesn't mean you have to know thes things, but they might benefit you in the long run.

Content Writing

Content writing is where you write content for any number of things. It could be as an advertisement (which is where the line between content writing and copy writing blurs), for a website, or any other number of things. Often, content writing is less a category of its own, and more a type of writing that encompasses the various writing tasks of all of the other freelance writing categories.

 Someone who works in "content writing" should be able to do a wide variety of writing tasks, both to sell things and inform people of what someone or something does, amongst other things. In fact, almost all freelance writers will become content writers, because content writing can encompass all of the different fields and niches in writing. One of the few things that are exclusive to the field of content writing is website content. While it is true that some website content will also be technical or copy writing, people will almost always advertise for a "content writer" when they need materials written for their websites.

Technical Writing

Technical writing is also similar to both content writing and copy writing. I have already explained that content writing refers to any type of "content." The difference between copy writing and technical writing, however, is that while a copy writer will be writing in order to persuade you to do, feel, or purchase something, a technical writer will be explaining how something works, how to do something, or other things along those lines. Technical writing is done to be informative, rather than persuasive.

Technical writers must often be experts in their specific field or fields. Of course, this is not always the case, as almost any information that one needs to find in order to do technical writing can be found online. People who are hiring freelance technical writers, however, often prefer to hire someone who has at least a minimal amount of knowledge on the subject they need to be written about. It is rarely a must, however, but simply a preference. For example, if a person or company is looking to hire someone to write car related materials, then they would prefer to hire someone who is either an auto-mechanic (retired or otherwise), or who at least had a general understanding of cars and the way that they work.

If you are someone who is an expert in a certain field of study, or who is an avid hobbyist pertaining to a specific subject, then technical writing might be a good way for you to go. If you are a person who is striving to become a technical writer, then I would suggest (like in content and copy writing) that you try to get a basic grasp or understanding of SEO, HTML, and computer/internet functions. Again, it is not mandatory, but I believe it would prove to be beneficial to you and your freelance writing career.

Translation Writing

Translation writing is one of the few types of writing that not everyone can do. The only way you can do translation writing is if you already have a firm grasp on another language. When I say "firm grasp" I mean a really firm grasp. You must know how to speak, read, and write another language fluently. People who are bilingual would be perfect for this type of freelancing, and there isn't as much competition in this field as there are in others. It can also be done for almost any language, although the most common translations being asked for seem to be in Spanish, French, Dutch, and Turkish - at least, this is what I have most encountered in my own experiences.

Translation writing can also go hand in hand with other types of freelancing. In fact, most types of writings will go hand in hand with at least one other field. As for translation, the most common type of job being offered is basic translation. This means that the person who is hiring you will want you to take a text that is in English and translate it into a foreign language. Or, on the other hand, take a text that is written in a foreign language and translate it into English. This isn't always the case, however. Occasionally, a person or company may want to hire someone who can write their own article and translate it into one or more languages on their own. Typically, the second job mentioned will pay more, since it is a harder job to do.

BLOG WRITING

Blog writing is also known as just "blogging." This, along with article writing, is one of the most common types of freelance writing. In fact, people who hire a "blogger" will often hire the same person to do both blog and article writing. But there are some major differences between the two, which is why I have decided to list them separately.

If someone hires you to do a blog, they will either want you to write on your own blog about them or their company or maybe even a specific service of theirs, or else they will want you to "ghost blog." When you ghost blog, you are writing a blog that someone else will sign their name to and that someone else (usually the person who has hired you) will post on their own blog.

Blogs are usually fairly brief. Meaning that, on average, they are written to be under 350 words or so. There are a few exceptions to the rules, of course, but this is a fairly accepted average. Blogs are also written in the first person, and are meant to be more relaxed and personable. Your personality or the personality your employer wants you to "pretend" you have should show in your blogs.

Article Writing

If you are hired to do article writing, then you will be writing or "spinning" articles. Writing articles is fairly self explanatory. When you "spin" an article, you are taking an original article and rewriting it so that it is no longer plagiarized. There are actually software programs you can purchase to spin an article, and about half of employers would prefer you to have it. The other half demands that you rewrite them yourself. Some people will want you to write an article, and then spin it a given number of times in order to come up with a variety of articles based upon the same exact subject.

Articles are written to be placed on a person or company's blog, website, or on other major websites or forums. This may be done for Search Engine Optimization purposes, informative purposes, or in order to back-link a person to an original article. Sometimes articles are written simply to build your employer's or their website's credibility.

Articles are typically longer than blogs are. On average, they will be no less than 350 words, and typically range up to 1,000 or 1,500 or so words. Some people may want even longer articles, but again, there are always exceptions to every rule in the freelance writing industry. Other ways that articles will differ from your average blog is that articles tend to be written in either the second or third person, and are a bit less personable, leaning more towards the formal side of things.

Creative Writing

Creative writing is a lot like indie publishing, but on a much smaller scale. Indie publishing is also known as "Independent Publishing," or "Self Publishing." That is when you publish your own book either as an ebook or a printed book, without the help of a major publishing company.

The only major issue that I have found that most people have with freelance creative writing is that more often than not, it is work for hire. This means that you retain no copyrights to your own materials, and will receive no profit in the event that it is sold or published, even if it becomes a huge success. Some people will allow you to put your name on your work as a co-writer or co-author. This is fairly rare, however, as the people who have contracted you for the creative writing job wish to gain credibility of their own. Obviously, they wouldn't want to share this with you, even if you did all of the work. Typically, you will be told ahead of time if you will be allowed co-rights. The easiest way around not wanting someone else to take credit for all of your hard work, however, is to simply refuse a contract or to not do this type of work.

Creative freelance writing ranges among all types of subjects and materials, from children's book to romance novels to adult fiction stories. If you have a high level of imagination, or enjoy creating stories of your own, and don't mind someone else taking credit for your work, then creative writing might be a good choice for you.

Chapter 5 - Decisions That Need To Be Made Before You Actually Begin

So now that you have decided what type of writing or multiple types of writing you will do, you need to decide a few other, very important things, before you actually get down to doing your freelance writing. Below are the questions you now need to ask yourself, along with explanations and/or suggestions as I feel is necessary.

Will You Work Full Time Or Part Time?

There are a lot of people who will only do their freelance writing part time. A good example would be a college student or a stay at home mom. The college student may do it on the side and in-between classes in order to have a little extra cash on the side without giving up a large part of their social life. A stay at home mom might do it in her free time to help pay her family's expenses, even if her husband makes enough money to support the family on his own. Then there are some people who prefer to work full time. This could be anyone, including the above mentioned college student or stay at home mom. To figure out which is best for your own situation, you need to look at two things. First, look at how much money you need to make to fit your goals, and second, take a look at how much free time you actually have to dedicate towards your freelance writing career. Let's go a little further in detail with these two items.

First: How much money you need to make to fit your goals. You should know that the starting wages for a freelancer with no major qualifications and no solid experience (either online or in person/on the job site) might only be between $1 and $3 an hour. At 20 hours, that means you will only make between $80 and $240 monthly. These rates will undoubtedly increase as time progresses and you gain experience (both in years and terms of jobs actually done). In fact, freelance writers with a good bit of experience under their belts (and perhaps a few online classes or certificates to boot) can make between $20 and $25 an hour! At just 20 hours a week, that is an additional income of $1,600 to $2,000 a month! That's no chump change! In fact, the vast majority of people could pay their rent and utilities with that amount of money! The most important thing for you to remember is that you just need to stick things out, keep your rates reasonable (based upon experience and schooling), and work your way up from the bottom. It's rough at first, but it will almost certainly pay off in the long run.

Before moving on to the second thing I talked about, I'd like to explain a few other things about a freelance writer's salary for a moment. When working online and at home (as the majority of freelancers do), you don't have gas money that you need to pay. If you are a parent, you don't have to pay for any kind of child care. There are no "added expenses" except for the internet, which will cost you no more than $60 a month if you shop around. So, if you ever feel down in the dumps about how little you think you are making, you can think about the fact that you are saving money. Think to yourself: well, it would normally cost me at least $20 a week to commute back and forth to a regular job, and I would have to pay around $100 a week for child care. Hey, look at that! If you add your savings onto your salary, you're starting out making $560! Maybe not literally, of course, but it should make you feel that much better. Remember: the pay can be fantastic. You just have to work for it.

How Much Time You Have That Can Be Dedicated To Your Freelance Writing?

All you need to do to figure this out is take a hard look at your schedule. Let me show you how to do this. For explanation purposes, we will look at a stay at home mom's schedule (since this, obviously, is the one I am most familiar with - I am a stay at home mom, after all). If this mom wakes up at 6:30 every morning, and goes to sleep at 9:30 every night, that leaves 15 hours a day open to work with. That is her "base" time, because that is how long she is awake. Yet, obviously, she has prior responsibilities and wouldn't want to work 15 hours a day, 7 days a week anyways. Now, we have to look at what she actually does and what times she wants for herself because everyone deserves a little free time.

 This mom decides that she doesn't want to work for the first hour that she is up, as she likes to enjoy a few moments to herself as she wakes up for the day. You know: nice pot of coffee and the newspaper or whatever it is she does. For the second hour that she is awake, she needs to get her children off to school. By 8:30 in the morning she is ready to work. This same mom, however, has decided that she would rather not work after her children arrive home from school, so she needs to end any writing jobs by around 3 in the afternoon. She would also like to take 30 minutes for a modest lunch break and brain relaxer. She will also need to spend one hour somewhere within that working time frame to tidy up her house before her family arrives back at home. We now know that this means she is able to work for six hours a day, five days a week (as she doesn't want to work on the weekends when her children are home). This stay at home mom is able to work 30 hours a week, which is considered full time. Anything beneath 30 hours is considered part time, while anything at or above is considered full time. Figuring out your own hours is as simple as you just witnessed.

Do You Wish To Work On Site Or At Home?

Generally speaking, most freelancers will choose to work at home. You get more job options this way, and you get the freedom of schedule that freelance writing offers. A few people, however, will decide to work on site. People who choose to work at a job site are typically the ones who have gone to college for writing or English or what have you. This isn't always true, but I have found it to be true for most people. If you want to work on site, this isn't really the guide for you, although you can take my guidelines and mold them to your own uses. If, like most people reading right now, you decide to work online, continue reading because that is exactly what this guide is for.

Time Shift Offer

Most people take up freelancing (in any form, not just writing) because they need more freedom in their schedule. If this is you, then you wouldn't want to take on a job that has you on a set time schedule. Some people simply enjoy writing and are able to work on a set daily or weekly schedule and be perfectly content in the process. The option you choose depends entirely on you and your own personal situation.

Are You Comfortable Working With Adult Materials Or Sites?

This is just something that you need to think about, since there is quite a bit of freelance work to be had that deals exclusively with adult content and materials. This does not mean, of course, that you will need to pose for nude pictures or host a naughty web chat. Sometimes people are just looking for independent contractors that can write copy for adult sites, or who can write romance stories with an underlying adult theme. If you are not comfortable with this, then you do not have to do this type of work. If you aren't sure, think about whether or not you blush every time a person uses a word that refers to someone's sexual organs. If you do blush, then this isn't the type of job for you. If not, then go ahead and try. If you are sure that you are comfortable with this type of work and content, however, than there will be a few more work options available to you.

On-The-Job Training

I highly suggest that you answer "yes" to this question. If you say "no, I am not willing to do this," then you shouldn't take up freelance writing, as it will never pay off for you. See, many people and/or companies are willing to take on "newbies." Newbies are people who have no formal training or experience. As such, they offer "on-the-job" or "as-you-go" training. This is usually done from the comfort of your own home, throughout the first few jobs they ask you to do. If you wish to take it one step further by broadening your education on your own, there are sites that offer free online classes. One of the best sites that I have found for this is called Alison.com.

Taking Free Class

Some people will already possess the knowledge and skills necessary to begin immediately. If not, I suggest online classes, as I mentioned in the question above. A few things that I believe would prove to be beneficial to you (and that I suggest you get a basic grasp on before you begin your freelance writing career) are: Search Engine Optimization (SEO), social media marketing, blog and article formatting, press release writing, and typing (to increase your words per minute if nothing else).

Do You Have Self Discipline To Be "Self-Employed"?

This is the last question, but it may also be the biggest, not to mention the hardest to answer. Here's the thing: Freelance writers are basically self-employed, no matter that they work for other people. You are the one who will actually set your own schedule, or find time to dedicate towards your career. No one else is going to do it for you. Some people will thrive under this freedom, while there are others who will just not be able to do it. If you believe that you will work well under your own management, and are disciplined enough to make sure that all of your work gets done, then you will do great in freelance writing. If you do not think so, then you need to go back to your day job, because you will go nowhere in the world of freelance.

Also try to remember that there is always stress involved in any job. It's no walk in the park, although I can vouch that it is a lot better than having an awful boss breathing down your neck every second of every day. The most important thing to remember is that you are now the boss and you are now the worker. Anything and everything falls on your shoulders, and no one else shares the burden. This is the biggest stress inducer when you work in the freelance writing industry, to be perfectly honest. Most people can handle it. If you can't, don't waste your time.

Chapter 6 – Putting Your Decisions Into Action

No matter what your decisions have been, what type of writing you would like to pursue, or whether you have decided that you want to work full time or part time, you will end up taking the same path towards implementing these writing decisions. The only way that you can do this is by becoming an independent contractor. By definition, an independent contractor is a person who is hired out by a single professional person or an entire company (could be a large or small company, it does not matter) to do one specific job or one set of similar jobs. The job that needs to be done could be long term or short term.

As always, there are things that you must consider during this step of the freelance writing process. But the first thing you need to do is get yourself out there. The best way to do this is through a professional platform that has been created to connect independent contractors with the people who want to hire them.

A professional platform is not simply the best way to do this, but the only way I recommend. I have tried striking out on my own, and it just does not work. The best (and one of the only) professional platforms is called oDesk. It allows you to search through jobs in order to find the ones you would like to do. On top of this, it allows professionals to search through contractor's profiles in order to find appropriate candidates for the jobs and positions that they need to fill.

Why would I suggest online going through a website like oDesk to do your online freelance writing? It's simple. They offer you a vast amount of job security. But what does that mean? Basically, it means that you are guaranteed payment for the work that you do, that you have someone to intervene as a mediator if you there is a dispute between you and another party, and that you have a much higher chance of actually getting a job in the first place. This isn't to mention that you will also find everything easier - from getting your first job and establishing yourself, to finding your niche or niches, all the way to becoming a huge success in the freelance writing world. Everything is made easier for you. All of the things that I have just mentioned are extremely important, especially if your freelance writing is supposed to support you entirely and not just supplement your income.

 In this stage of the process, there are two questions you need to ask yourself What period of time would you like the job to last? What type of commitment would work best for you?

As a freelance writer, your jobs can last anywhere from a few hours to indefinitely. If you don't care, then you can just look at the job itself and base your choice to apply or not apply on whether or not you will like the job itself (and do well at it) versus the amount of time that job will last. If you prefer to have only small commitments at a time, however, then you should go for the jobs that have a shorter time frame. For example, a simple job that will last no longer than a week. If you have decided that you would prefer something that would offer you more stability with more steady work, then you should look for jobs that will last for a longer period of time. For example, three months or more.

How Much Will You Charge For The Work You Do?

You need to be reasonable in the amount of money you plan to charge. When you first start out, I would honestly suggest charging a ridiculously low amount, at least for your first job. With no experience, it's unlikely someone will hire you without a really low fee. You can raise your price after the first job or two. The low rate is just so you can get a bit of experience under your belt. My very first freelance writing job paid only $3 an hour. The exact amount you end up charging is up to you, however.

You also need to think about the way you would like to be paid, as there are several different options. The most favored way by far is by the hour. This is typically a more secured way (on oDesk hourly payments are one hundred percent guaranteed). But you can also choose to be paid one lump sum per job or by the word or by the number of words you write. You can even choose to be paid by each article, blog, or other writings you do. Some people don't really have a preference, or else they prefer one option but will be paid by other options. For example, I prefer to be paid by the hour for the work that I do, but I have often taken on jobs of all the other varying ways to charge, since that was how the people or company preferred to pay.

Chapter 7 – Creating Your Online Presence

The next step, and perhaps one of the most important you will have to do, is creating your online presence. As I mentioned before, most people will work online. In the real world, you can simply walk into a room and establish a presence by being professional dressed or suitably mannered. Online things are just a bit tougher. You basically have to prove yourself to your perspective employers before you ever even begin working. The way you are able to do this is by creating a strong profile. This is yet another reason I suggest you use a professional platform like oDesk, which enables you to create and continue building a strong professional profile and portfolio. It is also done on these websites without too much hassle or effort on your part. I mean, some effort is needed, but why put forth more than you actually have to when you are just setting yourself up?

When creating yourself a profile, the first thing you need to do is list all of your qualifications. This includes previous jobs that are relevant to your freelance writing career, any schooling (including high school, in order to prove that you have a high school diploma or general equivalency diploma), and also any training or online classes that you have taken.

Once you have listed all of your qualifications, you will then need to create yourself a small but impressive portfolio. A portfolio is simply something that will show off some of the work you have actually done. If you don't have any previous work, just try writing something up. A short article or blog that you have just written will be sufficient to begin with. This will allow your perspective employees to see what you can do before they hire you.

Now you may go ahead and pick out a professional looking profile picture. While it isn't necessary, a profile picture gives your future employers a sense of knowing you. It puts a "face" to the name, figuratively as well as literally. When I say "professional looking" picture, I don't necessarily mean that it had to be professionally taken. You shouldn't choose a picture that has other people in it besides you. You should be the only one in the picture, and preferably it will just be a close up of your face, or from the shoulders up. Don't choose a picture that has been "MySpace angled" either. Just select (or take) a nice, clear shot of your face. Make sure that you are smiling, and that you look friendly and professional.

If you took my advice and are working oDesk or a similar site, then you will now want to take a couple of hours out of your day to take a few tests. This is so that you can prove your abilities. Some employers may require that you take these tests in order to do a specific job for them, and if you get a head start, you will already meet some of these people's qualifications. There are a vast number of tests that you can take. Feel free to try all of the ones you believe will be or even might be relevant to your job. They will show up on your profile for everyone to see, except in the event you choose not to show a specific test because of a low score or personal preference. Tests are especially important if you are one of those people who are starting their freelance writing career from scratch, with no relevant job experience or schooling. You might know that you are a good writer, but tests are the only way that you are going to prove your mettle ahead of time.

The last thing that you need to do when you are creating your profile is to set your price per hour, even if you have decided you want to be paid in a different way. This is the only price oDesk and other similar platforms allow you to set. It will be the basis for all other types of payments as well, so don't worry too much. You should start out low, like we have already discussed previously, and slowly raise your amounts as your prove to the online business world that you have what it takes to succeed. You will also be proving that you are worth paying a higher price.

Now, even though I said that was the last step, it isn't really. It's just the last thing that you have to do right now. The rest of your profile will really be built up later. On platforms such as oDesk, the people that you work for can leave you a rating. Any work that you have done via that website will be shown on your profile, along with the rating you received, and any comments your employer left you. People will also be shown on your profile how many hours you have logged via the platform. The more hours you have, the more knowledge you have in your specific subject (i.e. freelance writing), or at least that is what is assumed.

Right beside the number of hours you have logged, there will be an overall score based upon the ratings each individual person has given you. This will be the average of all of the individual scores you have previously received. These two things are very important, and they are two of the first things anyone will look at when they are thinking about hiring you. Why? These are two things that you cannot simply create yourself, therefore, these are things on your profile that cannot be forged in any way. You have to actually work in order to log hours, and you have to work well in order to earn a good score. This is why it is imperative that you also strive to do your absolute best on every job you do. Once dropped, your average score can be very hard to increase again. With a low score, it will be very hard for you to gain more hours, since no one will want to hire someone with a bad rating.

Chapter 8 – Applying Jobs

Now we are ready to start applying to jobs and responding to job offers. Chances are that you won't have any job offers just yet, but you will later, so I am going to cover them both. Keep in mind that you do not have to apply to all of the jobs that you see. In fact, you should only apply to the jobs that either interest you, you are actually qualified for, and/or that you have the time to do. This being said, you can and should apply to several different jobs. This is because the chances are very high that you will not be getting all of the jobs. In fact, you will probably only be hired for one out of every five or so jobs you apply for. Your odds might be better or worse, but this is a fairly good estimate for you to base your guesses upon. It is for this reason that I suggest bidding on ("applying to") somewhere between five and ten jobs to being with. Once you have checked that you meet all of the employer's qualifications, you can press the apply button. You will then be taken to a page that asks you to place a bid on the job and to write a cover letter.

Bidding On The Job

Here is an important thing for you to know. First of all, you can change your hourly wage or lump sum amount for every job, but remember not to bid too much higher than what you have listed on your profile. Your future bosses can see that price, and are more likely to shoot down your job offer if you raise it too much on them.

Also, don't be afraid to "outbid" the other people who are vying for the same job. When you "outbid" someone, you lower your rates to better your chances of getting the job. Just remember that you should never outbid someone by too much, as it is considered to be rude and unprofessional. You will see an average rate for the contractors who have already applied to the job. If that rate says $3.50 an hour, then don't be afraid to bid as low as $3.00. If it is a lump sum job, try not to bid more than $20 beneath the average. For example, if the average lump sum amount previous contractors have bid on the job is $50, don't go under $30. Honestly, if it were me, I would not go under $40. That is your own personal decision, however, like just about anything in freelance writing.

Now that you have successfully decided on and placed your bid, it is time to move on down the screen where you will write your cover letter.

Writing Your Cover Letter

Although you should always write a relevant cover letter for the job you are applying to, there are a few basic rules or guidelines to writing this important material. You need to remember that your cover letter is basically a self marketing tool. You need to market yourself like you would a product, and you need to think of the person you would like to hire you as the potential buyer.

Let me start by telling you one super important thing. Under NO circumstances should you EVER copy and paste a generic cover letter. A lot of people think it is perfectly appropriate to do this for every job that they apply you. I am here to tell you that it is NOT appropriate under ANY circumstances. Each cover letter you write should be written individually, and you should take your time to write a proper, professional one every time. I think I've made myself clear. Now that I've pounded that into your mind, let me explain why you should never use a copy and paste generic cover letter. The first reason is that it is considered very unprofessional and very rude. The basic thought behind this is "oh, they can't take enough time to write a proper cover letter? They must not really want this job." In addition to those main reasons, the other reason is that generic cover letters are considered to be spam through all major communication routes that are available to freelance writers.

Proper Cover Letter

The very first thing you need to do is to write a warm, yet professional greeting. Things such as "Hello Mr. John Doe," or "Hi Mrs. Jane Doe," are completely appropriate. "To whom it may concern," is a bit too formal, but is appropriate if there is no name under the job description or if it is a company that signed off on the job description instead of a single person.

The following phrases are not appropriate greetings for your cover letter under any circumstances: yo, dude, what's up, hola, or any other slang term.

Remember: You are a writer! Freelance or not, you need to present yourself as a reputable business professional. Throwing out slang terms as the first thing people will read simply makes you look like an uneducated street hoodlum. It might be an acceptable thing to do with your friends, your family, and people on the street, but it is not acceptable in the business world, where education rules and manners are key. You may not think the way you start your cover letter is that important. I mean, it's only a few little words, right? Yes, you are right. But they are the very first words your perspective bosses are going to see. If they don't keep reading, the rest of your cover letter will not matter one iota.

Now that we've covered the greeting, we need to talk about the "meat" of your cover letter. It's important to get straight to the point. The first thing you should do is tell the person or company why they should choose you for the job, followed by any qualifications or experience that you have to back it up. Only list relevant reasons. For example, if you went to college to become an auto-mechanic, but the job is for something fashion related, you wouldn't list it. If it was car related, then you would. See what I mean? It is also very important to address any specific questions that the employer asked to be addressed. Most people will simply throw away or delete applications that do not address specific questions or concerns like they asked you to do.

Now you need to close your letter. Good closers are "Best Regards," "Thank You," "Looking Forward To Hearing From You," and other things along those lines. A few examples of what not to write is "Yours," because it is too personal; "Love," because it's highly inappropriate; "Peace," because it's too laid back; or any other term along those lines. A good closer will wrap things up in a nice, professional way. After your closer, sign your name.

The very last thing you need to do is to attach a piece of writing that you have previously done. Make sure that it is relevant to the job position itself. If you are applying to a job that is asking for a content writer, then you should attach website content that you have written. If it is a job position for an article or blog writer, than you would attach your best article or blog. If you have something that is similar to the subject of the work they are asking to be done, attach that, even if it is not your best work. Just as long as it is good work, it is better to attach something based upon a similar subject. Then, you can press send and hope that you get the job.

Once you get a job, it will be time to move on to step six, which could be considered the real start to your freelance writing career!

Responding To Job Offers

Applying to jobs and responding to job offers are similar. The difference is that instead of making a bid, you need to accept a bid that has already been offered to you. Usually, this will be the hourly amount listed on your profile, but it will sometimes differ. The other difference is a few small variations to your cover letter. Instead of telling them why they should hire you, you need to tell them that yes, you will accept the job, and simply address any questions or concerns they might have. If they ask you what your qualifications are, or if you have some experience you have not yet listed on your professional profile or put into your portfolio, you may include it. Just remember to be brief.

Keep the greeting and the closer the same. The exact same set of rules apply to your greeting and closer when you are responding to job offers as when you are writing your cover letter and applying for a job position. It is only the "meat" or main portion of the letter that needs to change at all, and even that does not change much.

That's all there is to responding to job offers. It is much simpler than applying, but remember that you still might not get the gig, so don't be too upset if you don't. Just because a person or company has contacted you does not mean you automatically get the job. They may have contacted a small or large number of people that they were considering, and in the end, you may lose out to someone with a higher amount of experience or a lower price.

Chapter 9 - Getting Down To Business/ Beginning Your Freelance Writing Career!

Finally! Now you get to actually do some serious freelance writing work! This step is fairly simple and self explanatory. All you need to do is follow your employer's instructions to a T and work very hard. Try your best, and make sure that you keep in touch with your employer in whichever way they have told you is best for them. Regular communication is a key factor in completing a job successfully. Your employer will want to know where you are in your work, so that they can plan ahead to when the work is completed. Try to email (or call or Skype) your employer at least once a day, even if it is just to let them know how much progress you have been able to make throughout the day. Also make sure to contact your employer with any questions that you may have.

The most important thing for you to do is make your client happy. The easiest way to do this is to be polite and professional. Make sure that you always get your work done in the allotted amount of time (meaning: meet all deadlines), and that the work you submit is all the best work you could do in that amount of time. Don't ignore emails or phone calls from your clients, because this will only make them angry. If you keep your client happy, there is a good chance that they will come back to you if they have more of the same type of work in the future. Return clients are also more likely to pay you better. Build a strong business relationship with your clients, especially if you enjoy the work that they have for you to do.

When your job is finished, you can politely ask if you may include some or all of the work you have done for them in your portfolio. It's always okay to list an employer under your job experience, but it is necessary to ask before including work done for someone in your portfolio. This is because your employer usually retains all rights to your work, and they may not want it to be stolen or used again by anyone else. Most of your clients will allow you to include at least one piece of work in your portfolio, but don't be too upset if your client tells he would rather you didn't.

Chapter 10 - Continuing/Furthering Your Freelance Career

When each job or "contract" ends, you will receive a score that is based upon how well you did that job, possibly along with a few comments on specific things you did or did not do well. We've already gone over this, but remember that the more jobs you have, the more impressive a high rating is. Doing each job to the absolute best of your abilities is so important that I really can't stress it enough. One low score can ruin your overall rating, especially if you do not have many other jobs (and thus scores) already done.

As your hours logged in the oDesk application (or other similar platforms) goes up, you can increase your prices. Do not raise them too high. Compare your hours logged and your overall rating with the amount of money that you are charging.

Let us say, for example, that you began your career with an hourly charge of $3. You have been working for a little while, and now you have 100 hours logged. You have done three jobs, and your overall score rating is a 4.50. One hundred hours logged is pretty much your first big break, and a 4.50 is a pretty good score, even if it is not the absolute best score you could receive. (The best score is usually a 5.0 and that is the scoring I am basing this off of right now.) Instead of charging $3 an hour now, you could raise it to $3.50 or as high as $4.00 an hour.

I told you that it takes time and effort if you are starting from scratch. But let us say that you keep working, are truly diligently, take additional classes, do on the job training whenever you get the chance, and continue to get really good feedback scores because you do a truly excellent job. You are an all around great freelance writer, and it's not just you that know this, but the people who are doing the hiring as well. By the time you log in a thousand hours (and if you can keep your score up between a 4.0 and a 5.0), then you could reasonably be charging $10 to $15 an hour. Just remember: patience, patience, patience!

Besides the ratings, reviews, and salary, there are a few other ways that you can continue in or further your career. First and foremost, always take any opportunities that are offered to you (or that just happen along your way). Learn anything that you possibly can, and continue to take online classes in any subject matter you think may have even the slightest chance of helping you to further your career.

To be perfectly honest, the only way to really move your career forward is to do it yourself. When you are a freelancer, you are your own boss. This is great in a lot of ways, but it will never work out if you don't have the drive and ambition that is needed. You have to continually push yourself to do bigger and better things, to work more hours if it is needed, to rearrange your schedule if it is at all possible or necessary, and to take on as a large work load as you feel that you are capable of doing. Despite needing to push yourself, remember to never, ever take on more work than you feel you can comfortably manage.

Also try to keep your portfolio up to date. I mentioned before about asking a client if their work can be used in your portfolio, so I won't go over it again. When your work is allowed to be included, or if you do work on your own, make sure that you include it in your portfolio so that your perspective clients can see what you can do. You will always be improving your work and changing up your style. If an article or other writing project in your portfolio is no longer relevant to you, delete it. This is so important, because if your portfolio isn't up to date, then your employers may expect a certain style or a certain level of writing that they will no longer receive from you.

A Few Last Tips

Always put your best foot forward.

Do all of your work in a timely and efficient manner.

Make all communication with your employer brief and to the point, unless it is necessary or recommended by the employer themselves to do otherwise.

Never be rude to an employer, even if you feel like the employer is in the wrong.

Never lie in an application or cover letter in order to get a job; it will just end up backfiring in the end.

Don't take on too heavy of a workload, as this can cause the quality of your work to suffer. Don't charge outrageous prices, as you are much less likely to get hired when you do so.

Try your absolute hardest to meet deadlines . If you are unable to meet a deadline for whatever reason, let your employer know as soon as possible.

Give them a brief reason, such as: "I apologize for not being able to meet this deadline, sir. I had something come up, but I will finish it by "

Do not go into details, because honestly, they do not care. Try not to let it happen too often, either way.

Working Area

Never get discourage if you are not chosen for a job. More jobs will come along.

Try to keep meticulous records of your submissions, jobs, schedule, and anything else you need to make a note of.

Never be afraid to try and build strong working relationships with other freelance writers. This can prove to be beneficial to you in the long run.

Try to join professional organizations and attend workshops or conferences if you are ever able. This can help you to stay up to date with all freelance writing news.

Expect and understand any revisions or notes that your employer has for you. Learn from them, don't fume over them.

Remember that although you are technically your own boss, each person you work for is your boss for that small amount of time. Listen to what they tell you to do, and only offer your expert opinion if you really know what you are talking about. Even then, make sure that you do it in a way that is kind and professional, not rude.

An Ending Note

On a last note, I would like to wish you all of the luck in the world on your freelance writing adventures. I hope that you are able to take this guide and make it work for you and your situation in a way that will help you with your finances, fulfilling your dreams, both, or whatever reason it is that you have chosen to pursue a career in freelance writing.

I know that in the end it comes down to that old adage, "You can lead a horse to water, but you can't make him drink." I can only tell you what you should do, and explain to you what has worked for me in my own freelance writing career. In the end, it is up to you to implement the strategies outlined in this guide. I hope, more than anything, that you take my words and put them into action. Nothing would make me happier than to know you have created a successful freelance writing career (like my own) based upon what I have tried my hardest to teach you here today.

GOOD LUCK AND THE BEST TO ALL OF YOU

About The Expert

Chelsea Hammond has been a freelancer for roughly five years. She has worked primarily through the oDesk application when working for clients. She has done work in all fields of freelance writing, except for translation writing. The fields that she has the most experience in are blog writing, article writing, and content writing. On her own, she has also published one full-length novel ('A Severing of Ties'), and two books of poetry ('The Eloquence of A Child,' and 'A Rose Amongst Thorns').

HowExpert publishes quick 'how to' guides on unique topics by everyday experts. Visit <u>HowExpert.com</u> to learn more.

Recommended Resources

www.HowExpert.com – Quick 'How To' Guides on Unique Topics by Everyday Experts.

www.HowExpert.com/writers - Write About Your #1 Passion/Knowledge/Experience.

www.HowExpert.com/membership - Learn a New 'How To' Topic About Practically Everything Every Week.

www.HowExpert.com/jobs - Check Out HowExpert Jobs.

Printed in Poland
by Amazon Fulfillment
Poland Sp. z o.o., Wrocław

54640574R00034